IT'S BEEN A WHILE, RIVER NILE

THE MOST IMPORTANT RIVER IN ALL OF ANCIENT EGYPT

Ancient Egypt History 4th Grade Children's Ancient History

BABY PROFESSOR
EDUCATION KIDS

Speedy Publishing LLC

40 E. Main St. #1156

Newark, DE 19711

www.speedypublishing.com

Copyright 2017

In this book, we're going to talk about the Nile River, the longest river in the world and why it was important to the Ancient Egyptians. So, let's get right to it!

The Egyptians called the Nile River "Aur," which simply meant "black." As the river would flood the lands, it would leave behind fertile, life-giving, rich, black sediment. The river was named from the word "neilos," which in the Greek language translates to the word "valley."

Nile River

WHY WAS THE NILE RIVER IMPORTANT TO THE EGYPTIANS?

We think of Egypt when we think of the Nile River, but actually only about 22% of the Nile travels through Egypt. It's safe to say that civilization would never have started in the desert of Egypt if it hadn't been for the Nile River.

The Nile provided the Ancient Egyptians with everything they needed. It provided them with a way to grow food and to capture fish to feed themselves. It provided them with a transportation system, which they were able to harness once they built boats. It also provided them with building materials to create their homes and other buildings.

HOW LONG IS THE NILE RIVER?

The Nile is the longest river worldwide and it travels 4,160 miles (6,695 kilometers) across the land from south to north where it meets up with the Mediterranean Sea.

WHERE IS THE RIVER LOCATED AND WHAT IS ITS SOURCE?

The Nile River is situated in the northwestern section of Africa and winds its way through nine different countries. It's the major source of water not only for Egypt but also for Sudan.

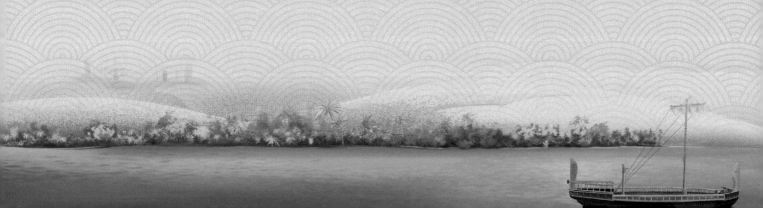

Nile River at the border of Egypt and Sudan

Lake Victoria

Two tributaries, the White Nile and the Blue Nile, feed it from different lakes. The White Nile's waters come from Lake Victoria, the largest lake in Africa, and other lakes in Central Africa. The flow that comes from the White Nile is regular throughout the year.

The Blue Nile starts in the mountains of Ethiopia at Lake Tana. Winds coming from the Indian Ocean cause annual monsoon rains that affect the Blue Nile. The water from these storms causes a massive water flow to go downstream, which is actually in a northerly direction.

Blue Nile

Khartoum City

The Blue Nile flows to the point where it meets up with the White Nile in the country of Sudan at the city of Khartoum, which is Sudan's capital. It takes rich, red sediment with it as it flows. Together these two mighty rivers join and flow north through Egypt to a vast delta that eventually ends in the Mediterranean Sea.

THE SEASONS OF THE NILE

Around the month of September on our calendar, the Nile would rage and overflow spilling into the surrounding lands. Floodwaters sometimes reached heights of 23 feet (7 meters). This would be disastrous today, but during those times they expected the flooding.

Aswan Dam

Today, the Aswan Dam built in 1968 prevents the floodwaters of the Nile from destroying cities. During ancient times, the flooding was a very important event because it was during this time that the soil was renewed by the silt deposits brought by the river.

The Nile's agricultural cycle had three distinct seasons.

AKHET

The word "akhet" means "inundation." This was the time of the year when the Nile was flooded. It generally occurred sometime between the months of June and September on our calendar. The Egyptians built canals to take the floodwaters to drier areas. During this time, no farming could happen so farmers generally went to work constructing temples or other buildings for the Pharaoh so they would have the money to settle their tax debts. They also mended their tools in preparation for the farming season.

Nile

PROYET

The word "proyet" means "emergence." This was the time of the year when the waters were at the right level for farmers to plant their crops. The temperatures were cooler than usual. The river had deposited a layer of thick, rich, black soil. The Egyptians called this Nile soil the "gift from the Nile." On our calendar, this time period was normally between the month of October and the month of February.

SHOMU

This season was summertime In Egypt. The dry season lasted from March through May. During this dry time, the farmers harvested the crops, so it was a very hectic time of the year. The tax collectors would show up during this time period to ensure that the Pharaoh received his share of payments. During this time, the irrigation canals were repaired in preparation for the next flood season.

Nilometer

MEASURING THE FLOOD WATERS

The Nile's flooding was somewhat predictable each year, but depending on the height of the waters, the results could be devastating. The Ancient Egyptians created a way to measure the annual flow. It was called a nilometer.

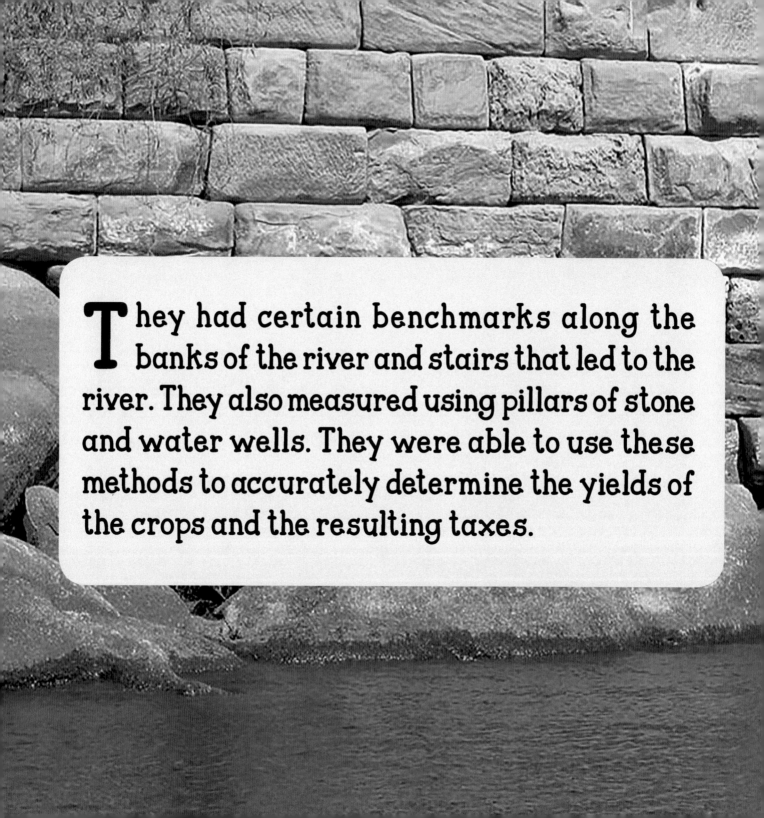

They had certain benchmarks along the banks of the river and stairs that led to the river. They also measured using pillars of stone and water wells. They were able to use these methods to accurately determine the yields of the crops and the resulting taxes.

WHAT DID THE EGYPTIANS PLANT?

The Egyptian farmers planted all different types of grains, vegetables and fruit, but there were three crops that were the most important.

WHEAT

In addition to using wheat as their main food to bake bread, the Egyptians sold their extra wheat throughout the surrounding countryside. This agricultural abundance made the Egyptians wealthy and it also made it possible for other roles within their culture in addition to farming.

Flax

FLAX

The Egyptians grew flax and they learned how to use flax to make linen fabric that could be used for their clothing. Most of their clothing was made from this type of cloth.

PAPYRUS

The papyrus plant grew wild along the Nile's shores. The Ancient Egyptians learned to cultivate it and they used it to create many different types of things. They made rope from it. They also made woven baskets and simple sandals for their feet. One of the most important products they made from it was an early form of paper used in scrolls.

Thebes

TRANSPORTATION ON THE NILE

During ancient times, transportation methods were limited and the Nile offered a way to get around by boat to transport goods back and forth. The trip from the city of Memphis to the city of Thebes took about half of a month during flooding or up to two months of time during the dry season when the waters were not flowing as rapidly.

The boats only traveled during the daytime, because the shifting sand deposits couldn't be easily spotted at night.

The boats were built with really shallow hulls so they wouldn't get stuck in silt in an area of the river that wasn't deep.

There were segments of the river that weren't passable by ship so they had to get out on land and travel to reach a segment that was passable again. When they were moving downriver the current carried them along, but on their travels upriver they would raise sails to help the wind propel them forward.

MATERIAL FOR BUILDING

In addition to being their source for food and transportation, the Nile offered them lots of mud. The Egyptians learned to use this mud to create bricks that could become like concrete when they were dried in the sun. They also used the river to transport limestone as well as sandstone that they had extracted from quarries. The Egyptians built the everyday home with mud bricks. The homes of the wealthy and the homes and tombs of the Pharaohs were built with stone.

Thebes, Upper Egypt

THE EGYPTIAN REGIONS: UPPER EGYPT AND LOWER EGYPT

At the beginning, Ancient Egypt was separated into two different regions. If you look at a map, you'll probably get confused about the position of Upper Egypt and its other section Lower Egypt.

The Nile River travels from south to north, which means that the Upper Egypt region was actually in the south because this corresponded to where the river began and the Lower Egypt region was in the north. The Lower region was where the river ended in the delta and then flowed into the Mediterranean Sea.

The two kingdoms came together around 3000 BC. However, each kingdom had its own color and headdress. Lower Egypt had a Red Crown, called a Deshret, and Upper Egypt had a White Crown, called a Hedjet. The pharaohs that ruled over both kingdoms wore a double crown, called a Pschent. One half of the Pschent represented Lower Egypt and the delta region and the other half represented Upper Egypt.

This red and white combination crown was also called a sekhemti, which meant "the two powerful ones." King Menes, also called King Narmer, united the two kingdoms. There is a major archaeological find called the Narmer Palette, which was discovered in 1897. It is a stone tablet that has engravings on both sides.

Narmer Palette

On one side it shows the king with the Deshret and on the other side it shows him wearing the Hedjet before the two types of crowns were combined into the Pschent.

It was the unification of these sections of Upper Egypt and Lower Egypt plus their rich resources due to the Nile River that made the civilization of Ancient Egypt so powerful and long-lasting.

Awesome! Now you know more about the Nile River and why it was important to the civilization of Ancient Egypt. You can find more Ancient History books from Baby Professor by searching the website of your favorite book retailer.

Visit

BABY PROFESSOR
EDUCATION KIDS

www.BabyProfessorBooks.com

to download Free Baby Professor eBooks
and view our catalog of new and exciting
Children's Books

Made in the USA
Columbia, SC
22 October 2020